"Father John ... f deep
faith and pr ... esence
of Christ to all of his ...... v book
of prayer that will bring us all closer to the Lord Jesus and
to our Catholic Church community."

FR. CECIL CRITCH, *Rector, the Basilica Cathedral of*
St. John the Baptist, Vicar General, Archdiocese of St. John's,
Newfoundland and Labrador

"This book is a unique opportunity for personal spiritual enrichment. Here, between the covers of one volume, Father Hillier provides an unparalleled collection of prayers that will assist in building an authentic Catholic spiritual life."

MOST REVEREND JAMES F. CHECCHIO, JCD, MBA
Bishop, Diocese of Metuchen, NJ

"What an incredible reminder that there is a prayer for every moment of our lives—from the tragic, to the joyous and even for the seemingly mundane (a prayer before a parish meeting, a prayer for a pet). Father Hillier's beautiful collection of prayers is a must in every serious Catholic's home library and a blessing for busy people looking for the perfect prayer quickly."

RACHEL CAMPOS-DUFFY, *TV Host*
SEAN DUFFY, *former Wisconsin Congressman,*
TV News Contributor

Good and Generous God

CATHOLIC PRAYERS FOR ALL OCCASIONS

REVEREND JOHN G. HILLIER, PHD

TWENTY-THIRD PUBLICATIONS

twentythirdpublications.com

*I dedicate this book
to my dear friend
and brother priest,
Reverend Monsignor
Edward C. Puleo*

IMPRIMATUR
Most Reverend James F. Checchio, JCD, MBA
Diocese of Metuchen, NJ

NIHIL OBSTAT
Reverend Monsignor Edward C. Puleo
Censor Librorum

May 17, 2022

The Nihil Obstat and Imprimatur are official declarations that a book or pamphlet
is free of doctrinal or moral error. No implication is contained therein that those
who granted the Nihil Obstat and the Imprimatur agree with the contents,
opinions, or statements expressed.

TWENTY-THIRD PUBLICATIONS • One Montauk Avenue; New London, CT 06320
(860) 437-3012 or (800) 321-0411 • www.twentythirdpublications.com

Cover photo: © stock.adobe.com / shintartanya
ISBN: 978-1-62785-710-9

Printed in the U.S.A.

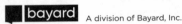

bayard A division of Bayard, Inc.

CONTENTS

|| PRAYERS WHEN FACING ILLNESS OR STRUGGLE

||| PRAYERS FOR FAMILY LIFE

IV PRAYERS FOR VARIOUS OCCUPATIONS

V PRAYERS FOR A PEACEFUL WORLD

FOREWORD

When Alfred Lord Tennyson of England wrote, "More things are wrought by prayer than this world dreams of" in the nineteenth century, little did he know that more than a hundred years later, people worldwide would continue to invoke his words. The meaning of these few words transcends time. They remind us, as well as people of every age, how very much our prayerful endeavors help enhance, transform, and accomplish a myriad of circumstances and situations when all natural efforts fail.

In addition to being guided by the inspired word of God in sacred Scripture, *Good and Gracious God: Catholic Prayers for All Occasions* by Father Hillier acknowledges the sentiments of Lord Tennyson in every page. Seeking to accommodate most every predicament, including vocations in life and difficulties that we encounter, he shares with us a prayer that will likely match our present need.

Over the years, Father Hillier has written hundreds of prayers for individuals and groups, including for parish and civil events. Some of his prayers have even been memorized for daily use by friends and strangers. In these pages, he shares many new prayers that will likely bring comfort and joy to people of all ages. Like Tennyson, he believes that "more things are wrought by prayer than this world dreams of"—or, as we are reminded by Jesus, "whatever you ask for in prayer, believe that you have received it, and it shall be yours" (Mark 11:24).

REVEREND MONSIGNOR EDWARD C. PULEO
Episcopal Vicar for Clergy and Consecrated Religious
Diocese of Metuchen, NJ

INTRODUCTION

Long ago, as a child in fourth grade, I recall collecting favorite prayers and poems and compiling them into a homemade booklet that I created using white scrap paper discarded by my dad. Using red and blue construction paper, I cut blue letters for the name of my "book" and pasted them onto the red front cover to await the collection that I began typing on my dad's old Remington typewriter.

In addition to my favorite prayers like the Guardian Angel Prayer and the Memorare, one of the poems in my collection was called "Trees," by Joyce Kilmer: "Poems are made by fools like me, But only God can make a tree." Another was from "In the Bleak Midwinter" by Christina Rossetti: "What can I give Him, poor as I am? If I were a shepherd, I would bring a lamb; If I were a Wise Man, I would do my part; Yet what can I give Him: give my heart." A third was a selection from the Book of Exodus: "Everything that the Lord has spoken we will do" (Exodus 19:8).

Little did I know as an eight-year-old that I would be doing something similar all these years later. This time, however, I am very much aware that I am unable to compose anything worthwhile without the help of the Holy Spirit. My words are limited, but when they are lifted up by God's Holy Spirit, they bear much fruit for the one offering the prayer, whether for themselves or for others.

I hope you enjoy this collection of prayers. My intention is to provide you with options for various needs and occasions. You may discover a particular prayer that you return to often, or you might seek a prayer for a particular need or circumstance as a one-time event.

This book is also a handy gift that you might choose to give a child or adult on the occasion of receiving one of the sacraments for the first time or to mark a birthday or special anniversary. Given the contents of this book, it is something I hope will become a keepsake for yourself or for others for years to come.

I take this opportunity to thank those who helped in the early stages of this project, including Joanne Ward, Shannon White, and Monsignor Edward Puleo.

REVEREND JOHN G. HILLIER, PHD

I

PRAYERS *for* OUR PARISH COMMUNITY

A PRAYER FOR OUR PARISH

Heavenly Father,
watch over our parish family
and help us to follow the example
of Jesus, Mary, and Joseph
as a model for our parish
and for all our families.

May Saint Joseph,
patron of the universal Church,
watch over our domestic church
and guide us in our decisions,
both great and small.

May Mary, model of the Church,
teach us true love,
help us become more virtuous,
guide us in our temporal affairs,
direct our spiritual well-being,
and intercede for us when all seems lost.

May Jesus, who gave us the Church
for our spiritual health and salvation,
hear us as we call out to him in prayer and
keep our parish family safe in his care,
protecting us from all evil,
both now and forever.

Amen.

A PARISH DISCERNMENT PRAYER

Jesus, our Savior,
so often we are overwhelmed
by the difficulties of life
and neglect to consider
the opportunities all around us
as a parish community.

Time has a way of passing,
and we easily miss the moments
given to us from your generosity
even as we gather in your name
to discern the needs of our parish.

Instill within us a renewed commitment
to make meaningful decisions
based on your eternal truth
that will direct us to live for you alone.

Help us, Lord, to trust in your divine will,
that we may give
all of who we are and what we do
to fulfill our roles
as members of our parish community.

Through Christ, our Lord,
Amen.

GOOD AND GENEROUS GOD

A PARISHIONER'S CALL TO SERVICE

God of love,
I come to you with an open mind and heart,
seeking to do your gracious will,
but am unsure how best to be of service
to you and your Church.

Stir up your Spirit within me now,
as I humble myself before you.
Help me to identify the best gifts
you have so generously blessed me with.

May I use my energy to activate these gifts
and place them at your service
for the people at my parish,
all for your greater honor and glory.

Amen.

PRAYER FOR A PARISH MEETING

Dearest God and Father,
as we gather in your name
to discuss matters great and small
pertaining to our parish,
fill us with the abundance of your Holy Spirit.

With the best guidance of your Spirit,
move our minds and hearts,
that we may place all the needs of our parish
before you and each other in a spirit of holy surrender.

Help us to seek only the good and the holy—
gifts that come from the heart of your Son, Jesus.
May the best of ourselves
become apparent in our present deliberations.

We desire the best for our parish
and ask only your helping hand
in allowing our voices to be heard
and our acts to be blessed,
so that both might be used
to draw others into this body of Christ.

Amen.

A PRAYER FOR HOPE AND COURAGE AMID A VIRUS

God our Loving Father, comforter of the afflicted,
watch over us always, but especially at this,
our time of urgent need.

With heavy hearts we cry out to you...
We ask that you heal those among us
who are weighed down with a virus.

Inspire with your holy wisdom
our health professionals: scientists, doctors,
and all medical personnel.
Show special attention to our government officials:
national, international, and local.
Make them instruments of your love
as they seek to serve your people.

Lord and Giver of Life, trusting in your mercy,
we recall the prayer of your prophet Jeremiah:
"Heal me, O Lord, and I shall be healed;
save me, and I shall be saved" (17:14).

When we are fearful, grant us courage.
When we are uncertain, strengthen us.
In our sorrow, comfort us.

With hearts overflowing with love for you,
we surrender ourselves to your providential care,
asking only that you consider our sincere request
to remain steadfast in your love—charitable to all
and faithful first and foremost in doing
your holy will.

Through Christ, our Lord,
Amen.

A POST-PANDEMIC PRAYER

Good and gracious Father,
send your Holy Spirit into our hearts,
that we may resume our lives
following the tragedies that beset our nation.

Help us to embrace your truth:

...that with Christ, there is peace even in war;
without Christ, there is war even in peace.

...that with Christ, the poor are rich;
without Christ, the rich are poor.

...that with Christ, adversity is sweet;
without Christ, prosperity is bitter.

...that with Christ, the ignorant are wise;
without Christ, the wise are fools.

...that with Christ, we commit ourselves
to the journey that leads to our Heavenly Father,
who gives us true peace.

Amen.

A SACRISTAN'S PRAYER

Loving Jesus,
I am grateful for the privilege
of being of service in your holy Church:
preparing the sanctuary,
cleansing the sacred vessels,
shining the brass candlesticks,
washing and ironing the altar linens,
arranging the vestments for your priests.

Create within me a clean heart,
that I may do all these things well:
first for your greater honor and glory,
as well as for your people who gather to worship.
May all who enter this house of God
find within, from the smallest to the most sublime item,
all things pointing to your profound love and majesty.

At the end of each day, Lord,
direct my thoughts to you alone,
that I may undertake the necessary tasks again tomorrow
to help myself and others worship well
and one day reach our heavenly home.

I ask this through your holy name,
Amen.

AN EXTRAORDINARY
MINISTER'S PRAYER

Jesus, my Lord and Savior,
you give us the gift of yourself in so many ways.
You are present to us in sacred Scripture.
You are present to us in your holy Church.
You are present to us through your own Mother.
You are present to us in the sacraments you gave us.

You are present to us most especially
in your Body, Blood, soul and divinity
in the Eucharist,
which you give us for our adoration
and spiritual nourishment.

May I be vigilant in the care that I give you, Lord Jesus,
in my liturgical role as Extraordinary
    Minister of Holy Communion.
Whether I am serving at holy Mass or visiting the sick
in their homes or at the hospital, may I remain solemn,
handling the Eucharist with utmost care,
with full knowledge and faith
that it is you who are present in the tiny host.

Amen.

A LECTOR'S / READER'S PRAYER

Jesus, our Lord and Savior,
Eternal Word of God made flesh,
watch over me each time
I reflect on your holy word
in preparation for Mass.

Called to proclaim God's holy word,
I desire to do it well so that all who hear
will be inspired to live lives of active love.

In my duty as assigned reader for holy Mass,
my desire is to utter every word
for your greater honor and glory.

May my heart overflow
with love for your word
and your Word made flesh in the Eucharist.

May the words that flow from my lips
reflect the best of who I am,
the fruit of my prayer and
the yearnings of my heart.

May my every motive be directed
by my deepest desire
to do all things according to your holy will.

In Jesus' name,
Amen.

GOOD AND GENEROUS GOD

AN ALTAR SERVER'S PRAYER

O my Jesus,
I am so grateful to be your altar server,
leading the priest to the sanctuary
for holy Mass.

As I stand and hold the Roman Missal
for the prayers addressed to our Heavenly Father,
I pray that my prayers, too,
may rise to the house of God.

Whether I am carrying the processional cross,
setting the chalice and paten on the altar,
ringing the bells, or
holding the vessels of wine and water,
may I never lose sight of the privileged function I serve
in assisting your priest to bring
your precious Body and Blood to the altar.

Before Mass begins,
help me set my thoughts solely on you.
After Mass,
may I whisper a prayer of gratitude
for your allowing me to minister in this way.

May I never take the Mass for granted
or the role I play in helping the people of God
to set their thoughts on you
and receive you in the host in Holy Communion.

Through Christ, our Lord,
Amen.

STEWARDSHIP PRAYER

God of love,
grant me daily the graces I need
to follow in the footsteps of Jesus.
Help me to trust in your love
and to grow in greater fidelity
and friendship with you.

I thank you for the trust
you place in me
as steward of the various gifts
with which you have blessed me.

May your Holy Spirit guide me
as I renew my commitment
to place my time, talent, and treasure
at the service of others.

As I seek to become a more faithful witness
of the saving riches of your Son, Jesus,
grant me the generosity, wisdom, and insight
to live according to your holy will
in all I am and all I do.

This prayer I offer through Christ, our Lord,
who lives and reigns with you
and the Holy Spirit,
one God forever and ever.

Amen.

A CATECHIST'S PRAYER

God of endless charity,
look upon us in your kindness.
Shower us with your grace and love
as we seek to offer
the fullness of faith to your children,
our brothers and sisters in Christ.

May all who are called
to a deeper relationship with you
discover an abundance of joyful hope
as they seek to become your faithful disciples.

May our teaching apostolate
be that of helping to form and inform
those whom you beckon
to be counted among your chosen children.

May all our efforts,
after your example, Great Teacher,
help cultivate new disciples
who, in turn, may become
beacons of light and hope,
calling others to deeper faith and charity,
in imitation of you.

Through Christ, our Lord,
Amen.

A MUSIC MINISTER'S PRAYER

God of beauty and truth,
as King David sang your praises long ago,
with melodies of joy and hope,
so may we bring praise to your name
through the lyrics and melodies we sing and play
here at our parish of _____.

You have called us forward,
blessed already with a love and talent for music.
May all our efforts
be spiritually uplifting,
helping create a more prayerful environment
for your Church and for the people we are called to serve.

Pour forth your blessing upon us
and fill us with your love.
With our hearts and voices raised in song,
may we do our best,
all for your greater honor and glory.

Through Christ, our Lord,
Amen.

A PRAYER FOR GODMOTHERS

Father of all, you revealed yourself to us
as a loving and merciful Father
and gave the Blessed Virgin Mary to us
as a loving Mother.

May she be a model for all earthly mothers,
including godmothers who seek to imitate her
in their duty as stewards of our precious faith
in the life of the newly baptized.

May my faith grow and develop
into a beautiful gift,
especially because of the example
of my godmother.

Keep her secure in the knowledge
that you will continue to bless her,
as she has been a blessing to me.

May I always recall the joy I have experienced
because of my godmother,
especially a heart full of gladness
that you chose her to be a role model in my life.

Through Christ, our Lord,
Amen.

A PRAYER FOR GODFATHERS

God and Father of all,
you revealed yourself to us
as a loving and merciful Father.
Look upon all earthly fathers,
including godfathers who seek to imitate you
in their duty as custodians of our precious faith
in the life of the newly baptized.

May my faith grow and develop
into a beautiful gift,
especially because of the example
of my godfather.

Keep him secure in the knowledge
that you will continue to bless him,
as he has been a blessing to me.

May I always recall the joy I have experienced
because of my godfather,
especially a heart full of gladness
that you chose him to be a role model in my life.

Through Christ, our Lord,
Amen.

A PRAYER FOR A NEWLY BAPTIZED PERSON

God of all creation,
how grateful I am for the gift of my life.
My heart is overflowing with joy
as I seek only to do your will.

Born again through the waters of baptism,
I pray that I may never sway
from the abundance of love
you have bestowed upon me.

Allow me many opportunities
to fall prostrate before you.
Because you loved me first,
I seek only to adore you and serve you.

May my soul, filled with your grace,
constantly seek the broken and downtrodden,
so I may imitate our Lord Jesus
in service to you and my neighbor.

Amen.

A LAY MINISTER'S PRAYER

Jesus, my Lord and Savior,
I seek always your precious gifts
of faith, hope, and love—
not only for my own spiritual advantage
but also for the benefit of those
you have chosen to place in my path.

May those I meet each day
know the depth of your love for them
and love you, above all,
with their whole hearts.

With my attention fixed solely on you, Lord Jesus,
I ask for your special grace,
that I may move forward each day,
knowing the depths of your love
and seeking to share these heavenly treasures
with everyone I meet.

May my ministry always be dedicated
to you and for you.
If I benefit at all,
may it be only to move me onward
in sharing your love and grace,
so that others may see what I see
and grow in greater love of you.

In Jesus' name,
Amen.

A PRIEST'S PRAYER

Christ Jesus, our Lord and High Priest,
receive my prayer this day
as I go about doing your work
in the vineyard.

May I first and foremost be for others
a priest following your gracious will.
As I seek to imitate you each day,
may I offer others your immense mercy
and your boundless love.

In my private thoughts and prayers,
may I constantly hold up the people
under my pastoral care.
May those who have already passed from this world
remain in my prayers,
and may those now counted among the saints
intercede for us here below.

In your great love, Lord Jesus,
provide me daily with the priestly fervor
that I recall from the day of my ordination.
May I be your priest for others without ceasing.
May I do my priestly duties without complaint.
May I offer my priestly presence without recompense.
May I give my all for you and in imitation of you,
for your greater honor and glory.

Amen.

A PRAYER FOR DEACONS

Almighty and eternal Lord,
in your never-failing providence
you care for and strengthen
all who approach you in prayer.

Provide from your generous bounty
for all your deacons
and all who are discerning the call to the diaconate.
Following the example of deacons like Saint Stephen,
Saint Lawrence, and Saint Francis of Assisi,
inspire many to serve as deacons.

May your deacons love proclaiming the gospel
by word and example.
May they live the corporal and spiritual works of mercy
as instruments of faith, hope, love, and peace.

Grant that many lives will be inspired and transformed
by their example and their faith,
but most especially
their love for the poor, the sick, and the unwanted.

Keep them in your care always.
Comfort them by the words of sacred Scripture
and by your Eternal Word made flesh.

I ask this through our Lord and Savior Jesus Christ,
who lives and reigns with you,
forever and ever,

Amen.

A PRAYER FOR A BISHOP

God, our loving Father in heaven,
we praise you for the many gifts to your Church,
including the leadership of our chief shepherd,
to watch over and guide your diocesan Church.

Keep our bishop faithful to your holy word,
enabling him to love it and share it
among all people under his pastoral care.

Whether it be your word present in sacred Scripture,
or in the sacred Tradition of your holy Church,
may your word shared by our bishop
take root deep within our hearts.

Blessed Lord, may our bishop serve you well
all the days of his life.
May he be blessed with good health
as he seeks only to live your life through his
and then one day be counted among your saints
in the heavenly kingdom.

We ask this through Christ, our Lord,
Amen.

A PRAYER FOR THE POPE

All-good and generous Lord,
watch over our Holy Father,
and in your benevolence,
keep him in your care.

As we go about our daily lives,
remind us to share our Catholic faith
with conviction and charity,
following the example of our Pope.

Give us each day
the depth of your love
to pray for our leader
with an undivided heart.

Keep us focused on the mission of your Church,
that Christ may bless all keepers of the faith,
especially our Holy Father
when he teaches, preaches,
and lives God's love and mercy
for all to imitate.

Through Christ, our Lord,
Amen.

A PRAYER FOR MISSIONARIES

Good and gracious Father,
send many among the people of God
into mission territories that still await
your beautiful gospel of truth and life.

Watch over your servants—
priests, sisters, brothers, and lay faithful—
who carry your word and sacrament
as they care for those seeking
greater faith, hope, love, and mercy.

May your Holy Spirit
renew their commitment to you each day
as they seek you in prayer,
in those with whom they live,
and in the people they serve.

May their love for you grow,
their knowledge of you increase,
and their faith be unshaken
as they surrender themselves to you
and your Church
all the days of their lives.

Amen.

A PRAYER FOR PRIESTLY VOCATIONS

God, our loving Father,
open wide the hearts of our youth,
that young men may respond generously
to your call and consider priestly service
in your Church.

May they follow Christ,
the Good Shepherd,
who came not to be served but to serve
and to seek out and rescue
those who are lost.

May God's word be for them
a source of courage and wisdom.

May the Eucharist be
a source of strength and nourishment.

Prepare them, O Lord, that others
may find in their presence
the love and care of Jesus,
our eternal High Priest,
who is Lord for ever and ever.

Amen.

A PRAYER FOR PARISH VOLUNTEERS

Lord of all,
send forth many from your flock
to share the best of themselves
in our various ministries, great and small.

May those entrusted to share your gospel
be strengthened each day with your grace
to be powerful instruments of your love and mercy.

Bless your faithful who already volunteer in your vineyard,
that they may not become disillusioned
by those who seek a different cause than yours.

Sustain all volunteers, both new and old,
that they may never waver from your call
to give of themselves, all for your greater honor and glory.

Through Christ, our Lord,
Amen.

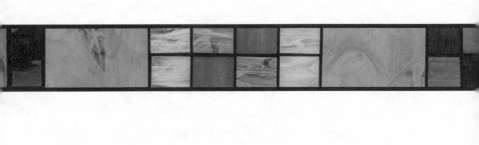

II

PRAYERS
When FACING
ILLNESS *or*
STRUGGLE

A PRAYER FOR ALL HUMAN LIFE

God of infinite love,
open wide our hearts and minds,
that we might be worthy advocates
for the voiceless and vulnerable.

Give us the courage of will
to remain vigilant to the unborn,
the generosity of heart
to offer support to the sick,
the constant desire
to be present to the elderly,
the abundance of love
to be committed to the disabled, and
the perseverance to seek and find
the lost and forgotten.

Lord and Giver of life,
in your love and mercy,
keep us safe in your care
as we strive to serve you.

May we always keep before us
the challenge to recognize
the face of Jesus
in all those we meet.

Through Christ, our Lord,
Amen.

A PRAYER TO HELP US CARRY OUR EARTHLY CROSSES

Good and gracious Father,
watch over us on our earthly pilgrimage
as we make our journey to you.

Bless us and all those who struggle
under the weight of a cross.
Make us worthy advocates and caregivers
for the voiceless and vulnerable.

Inspire us to embrace our crosses willingly.
May those who live with pain, disability, or
serious illness, or who feel misunderstood or betrayed,
use their suffering well by offering it in union
with your suffering on the cross at Calvary.

Instill within us the grace to embrace
our difficulties and hardships for love of you
and to invite others to do likewise.

Unite us to your Son, Jesus, through prayer
and sacrament, that we may cooperate
fully in your redemptive plan.
Use us in all ways, even in our suffering,
so that nothing is wasted but all is offered
for your greater honor and glory.

Through Christ, our Lord,
Amen.

A PRAYER FOR
BATTLING INSOMNIA

God of all,
how often I find myself in the quiet of the night
thinking of you and wondering how it is
that as Creator of the universe,
you have no need to sleep.

But, Lord,
I pray night after night for the opportunity
to move from being awake to falling asleep,
as Jesus once did in a boat in a storm,
among other places.

As the constant urge to remain awake
gnaws at me from the inside out,
I ask your intervention that I may rest
in the comfort of your divine presence,
both tonight and every night.

In Jesus' name,
Amen.

A PRAYER FOR HEALING

Jesus,
comforter of the afflicted,
watch over us always,
but especially in this,
our time of urgent need.

With total surrender to you
and your holy will,
we ask for your healing presence
to surround and penetrate
the body and spirit of our loved one.

Lord and Giver of Life,
as we trust in your mercy,
we recall the prayer
of your prophet Jeremiah:
"Heal me, O Lord, and I shall be healed;
save me, and I shall be saved" (Jeremiah 17:14).

With similar conviction,
we echo the sentiments of your prophet
and of your Church's prayer for healing.
With hearts overflowing with love for you,
we surrender ourselves to your prerogative
and ask only that you consider our sincere request,
first and foremost for your greater honor and glory.

Through Christ, our Lord,
Amen.

A PRAYER FOR A CHILD
WITH A DISABILITY

Lord of heaven and earth,
watch over this child
created in your image
but faced with difficult anomalies,
some discernible,
others not so visible.

On the more difficult and challenging days,
provide us with the strength we need to endure
and the grace to embrace your cross as well.

When times are less hectic,
and on the more difficult days, too,
give us grateful hearts.

Fill your child at all times, Lord,
with peace of mind, body, and spirit.

Keep us faithful always.
May our Blessed Mother watch over us,
and may all your saints protect us.

Through Christ, our Lord,
Amen.

A PRAYER FOR SOMEONE WHO
HAS EXPERIENCED CHILD ABUSE

God of all that is good,
giver of life and truth,
keep me safe from this day forward.

Protect me and all your children
from the grip of terror
that happens when evil,
disguised as good,
raises its ugly head
and steals all that is precious
from the most sacred places.

Help me to trust more, Lord,
especially when others have genuine motives,
wishing only to offer their love and support.

While much has been stolen,
I pray, with your help,
that nothing more will be taken.

When terrorizing memories haunt me,
may your grace, Lord Jesus,
enable me to place
all my trust and confidence
in you and you alone.

I ask this in your holy name,
Amen.

A PRAYER FOR
SUCCESSFUL SURGERY

Jesus, Lord of love and life,
be present to me
at this crucial time in my life
as I embark upon major surgery.

Squash my fears and anxieties
as you embrace me in your love,
that I may trust your will for me—
that I may remain safe and secure.

Give me the presence of mind
to ask all the right questions
to those responsible for my care.

Help me maintain the proper disposition
to show gratitude to all who care for me,
including the medical team,
caregivers, relatives, and friends.
May I never take any of these for granted.

Bless all who support your mission of love.
May they be embraced in the care
of your Mother, Mary,
and protected by the saints of heaven.

Amen.

A PRAYER FOR HOSPITAL STAYS

Lord Jesus, comforter of the sick and afflicted,
you have always watched over me
during times of good health and prosperity.

Be with me now in my time of pain and suffering,
especially as I wrestle with the fear
of my stay in the hospital.

As I face the unknown about myself—
the worry associated with my medical condition,
my wandering mind on sleepless nights,
the difficulty of diagnosis and prognosis—
comfort me, sweet Lord and Savior.

Give me the grace, O Jesus,
that I may offer my heartache
and all that consumes me
to help lighten the burden of other patients
who suffer more significantly,
so that, despite my plight,
even my sickness may bear much fruit
for your greater honor and glory.

Amen.

A PRAYER TO FIGHT CANCER

Dearest Lord Jesus, our divine Physician,
fill your servants with your healing presence
as they do their part to fight this horrifying
    disease within them.
Shine your healing power into their bodies, hearts, and souls.

With humility, as they seek your comfort and mercy,
allow the best of who they are as your followers
to remain optimistic for the sake of their families, friends,
and others they have yet to meet.

With the help of your Holy Spirit,
    remove all cancerous invaders
that have overrun their bodies, your temple.
Replace all deadly cancer cells with good, wholesome cells.

Aided by the powerful intercession of your heavenly helpers,
Saint Peregrine and Our Lady, Queen of Peace,
keep them steadfast in the hope
that "if you ask anything of the Father in my
    name, he will give it to you" (John 16:23).

In Jesus' name,
Amen.

+ Saint Peregrine, pray for us.

A PRAYER FOR A CANCER SURVIVOR

Dear Jesus, Lord of all,
with a grateful heart
I surrender myself to you.

As I reflect on the
blessings of my life,
I am keenly aware
of the new opportunities
that I have been awarded,
having survived cancer.

May I never take
the gift of my life for granted
or question the source
of this huge blessing.

Protect me
and my loved ones, Lord,
from the terrible
disease of cancer.

Bless those who have
journeyed with me
during these, the most difficult days:
nurses, doctors, caregivers,
pastoral ministers, family members,
friends, and so many others
known to you alone.

May all be embraced
through the gentle love
of your Holy Spirit.

Amen.

+ Saint Peregrine, pray for us.

A PRAYER FOR SOMEONE LIVING WITH MENTAL ILLNESS

God of all Glory,
as I find myself overtaken
by signs of mental illness,
I surrender myself to you for healing,
knowing that nothing is wasted in your divine plan.

May my days be filled with opportunities
to become more aware of my condition,
my limitations, and my abilities—
in short, the truth of my diagnosis.

Allow me, Lord,
with the help of your grace,
to have focused determination
to overcome all things that undermine
the core of my Catholic beliefs.

With conviction of heart
to become more assimilated
into the life of the Church,
I ask for your healing and help
to know what you want of me...
so I may do all according to your designs.

Through Christ, our Lord,
Amen.

A PRAYER FOR SOMEONE LIVING WITH ADDICTION

How painful it is, dear Lord,
to consider that I have
come to this place.
I am not only unrecognizable to others,
but often to myself as well.

Although I have slipped so far, so fast,
and now it seems impossible
for me to recover,
I believe, merciful Lord,
that you can provide me
with glimmers of hope
for a better tomorrow.

Grant me, Lord Jesus,
humility of spirit,
that I may find the
courage and determination
to remain focused on your holy will.

Keep me, God of love,
always hopeful,
filled with faith and charity,
more trusting toward others,
especially those who, deep down,
I know have my best interests at heart.

In Jesus' name,
Amen.

A PRAYER FOR THOSE
LIVING WITH MEMORY LOSS

God of love,
watch over our elderly
with care and compassion,
especially those living with
the effects of dementia,
including Alzheimer's disease.

Lord of life,
may your interior gift of peace
become an oasis of serenity
for those burdened by
the terrible cross of memory loss.

Keep safe all those challenged
by these mysteries that accompany old age.
May our presence with them
be marked by love, respect,
patience, and understanding.

With the passage of time,
may our faithfulness endure
and hope be rekindled
as we look forward to new opportunities
of becoming reacquainted one day
in the home of our eternal Father.

In Jesus' name,
Amen.

A PRISONER'S PRAYER

God of infinite mercy,
look down upon me,
your prodigal child,
on this day which seems
like every other day.

Sorrow remains my best friend,
which includes among its attributes
complete loneliness, mental anguish,
heartache, and hints of despair.

Only you, Lord, understand my heart,
my mind, and the depths of my soul.
Only you can comprehend
the intensity of the cross I bear.

I bow before you and beg your intercession.
Give me the strength of character
to accept what I cannot change
and to surrender fully to your providential care.

This prayer I offer through Christ, my Lord,
Amen.

A PRAYER WHEN FACING DEATH

Most gracious Father,
Lord of all,
watch over me and console me
during this time of wonderment and impasse.

As my life on earth comes to its natural end,
I wish to renew my love for you above all
and my love for others as well.

Help me, Lord Jesus, begin anew...
with sentiments of hope—
in the glory you have prepared for your children
before the foundation of the world.

O Holy Spirit of God,
although my life draws to a close,
remind me often how best I can serve you
until that day when I am safely home
in the house of our Heavenly Father.

In Jesus' name,
Amen.

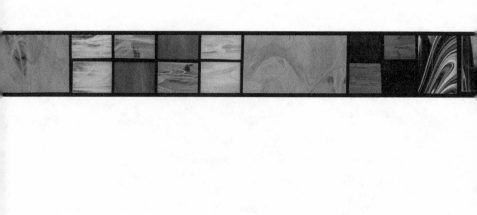

III

PRAYERS
for FAMILY
LIFE

A HOUSE BLESSING

God of love,
watch over us, your children,
and keep us in your care.

May we be blessed and protected
by all your generous bounty,
in the safety and security of our home.

Bless our house with your grace
and protect all who live here.
As we seek each day
to make our house a better home,
be present to us in all ways.

May all good things abide with us
and all evil be abolished.
Never allow the devil or his minions
to enter our home.

May your blessing be extended
to all we meet
and to all places we visit.
Keep us safe, Lord, always.

We ask, as we do all good things,
through Christ, our Lord.

Amen.

A PRAYER FOR YOUTH

Generous Father in heaven,
direct the abundance of your grace
deep within the souls of our youth,
that they may respond generously
to the life you call them to live.

May they follow daily your Son, Jesus,
learning from his life on earth,
seeking to imitate Christ always:
    ...the way they live,
    ...the way they love,
    ...the way they face new challenges,
    ...the way they act as his disciples.

May your holy word
inspire our young people
to new and more profound pursuits.
May your sacraments be for them
food for their journey and
nourishment for their spiritual lives.

Make them images of Jesus,
always giving of themselves,
for your greater honor and glory.
May others find in them
young, energetic disciples,
ready and willing
    ...to give rather than take;
    ...to love rather than hate.

All this we ask, through Christ, our Lord,
Amen.

A PRAYER FOR CHILDREN

Father, God of love, watch over our children.
Give them deep faith, abiding hope,
and everlasting love.

Jesus, Light of the universe,
shine forth your rays of truth
into the minds and hearts of our children.

Holy Spirit, Lord and Giver of life,
pour your divine love on our children,
that they may enjoy forever
the fruit of your affection.

Through Christ, our Lord,
Amen.

A PRAYER ON THE FIRST DAY OF SCHOOL

Jesus,
you spoke in the gospels
about loving the little children
and asking the children to come to you.

On this, my first day of school,
I ask that you be with me the entire day
as I leave home for the first time
and venture off to school.

Help me to be unafraid
as I say goodbye to my mom and dad
and go off to meet my new teacher
and all the other boys and girls
for the first time.

Help me be polite to all those I meet.
May I be kind to my classmates,
be respectful to my teachers,
and try my best to do all things well.

When the school day is done,
may I return home to my loving family,
thankful that you gave me a wonderful day
filled with new people to share with and care for.

In Jesus' name,
Amen.

A PRAYER FOR
AN EXPECTANT MOTHER

Gracious Mary, Mother of Jesus,
protector of all God's children,
we appeal to you during our time of need,
that you may throw your mantle
around the mother and child for whom we pray.

May the child in her womb find solace
in being held up in our prayer.
May this, and every child, like Jesus and John the Baptist,
realize the maternal care
with which they are so loved.

Always aware of God's special favors,
may the blessed one, Saint Gerard,
intercede, too, for this mother and child,
that they may find comfort and safety
in the intimacy they now share.

May the pain of childbirth be a reminder
that this child and every child
is worth more than money can buy,
because this new soul is destined
to be with God for all eternity.

Through Christ, our Lord,
Amen.

A PRAYER FOR
AN EXPECTANT FATHER

God, Father of love,
look upon this expectant father
and, in your goodness,
bless him as he prepares to receive his new child.

As you have done throughout the ages,
in the Old Covenant with Abraham,
and in the New with Zechariah and Joseph,
bless this man with a child he can call his own.

Give him the grace to be, with his wife, a good parent,
suited to the vocation of fatherhood,
that his might become a household with many souls.

Bless this dad in all ways,
that he may surrender himself to your will
all the days of his life.

In Jesus' name,
Amen.

A PRAYER FOR FAMILIES

Heavenly Father,
watch over our family
this day and every day.
Help us to follow the example
of Jesus, Mary, and Joseph
as a model for our family.

May Saint Joseph,
patron of the universal Church,
watch over the domestic Church of our family
and guide us in our decisions,
both great and small.

May Mary, model of the Church,
teach us true love,
help us become more virtuous,
guide us in our daily lives,
direct our spiritual well-being, and
intercede for us when all seems lost.

May Jesus, who gave us the Church
for our spiritual health and salvation,
hear us as we call out to him in prayer,
keep our family safe in his care,
and remain with us always,
both now and forever.

Amen.

A PRAYER FOR SPOUSES DESIRING A CHILD

God of love,
look down upon us and,
in your goodness,
bless our marriage and our love for each other.

As you have done throughout the ages,
in the Old Testament with Sarah and Abraham,
and in the New with Elizabeth and Zechariah,
bless us with a child we can call our own.

Give us the grace that we may become parents,
with minds and hearts suited to the vocation of
motherhood and fatherhood,
that ours might become a household of many souls.

Bless us, Lord, in all ways
as we surrender ourselves to your will.
Show us what we must do
to fulfill your request to "be fruitful and
    multiply" (Genesis 1:28).

In Jesus' name,
Amen.

A PRAYER FOR FATHERS

God, Father of mercy,
shine the abundance of your love
upon our earthly fathers.

Keep my dad in your care.
Give him the necessary strength
of mind, body, and spirit
to fulfill his many responsibilities
as custodian of our family.

When he is distracted by the circumstances of life,
give him hope and optimism.
When he is weighed down with torment,
give him interior peace.
When he is challenged by the details of worldly cares,
give him a share in your Fatherly comfort.

Father of all,
as my dad grows in age and wisdom,
grant him the grace to embrace more profound faith,
greater hope, and deeper love for you.

Keep my dad safe in your care, Heavenly Father.
Give him the grace of perseverance,
that he may remain faithful to you
and always in your loving embrace.

Through Christ, our Lord,
Amen.

A PRAYER FOR MOTHERS

Father of all creation,
be attentive to our mothers,
and hold them in your care.

As you once embraced
Mary, your Mother and ours,
giving her to us as our maternal advocate,
we ask that you watch over and
guide our earthly moms
with similar benevolence.

When they are distracted and weighed down
by the cares of motherhood,
grant our moms reprieve and respite.
When they are overwhelmed by distractions
and other obligations they must shoulder,
bless our moms with your confidence
and your comforting Fatherly support.

Through Christ, our Lord,
Amen.

A PRAYER FOR MARRIED LIFE

Good and gracious Father in heaven,
you give life to all good things
and make them holy.
How grateful we are
for your gift of holy matrimony—
joining man and woman as one,
all the days of their lives.

Your generosity is without end,
allowing those joined in marriage
to live life and share love to the fullest,
giving spouses the opportunity
to rediscover each other again and again;
sharing their love with one another
and with their children;
caring for their family, at times with sacrificial love
and even with crosses to bear.

May their hearts overflow with joy
when thinking about the simple gestures—
a spouse's affection, a smile, a twinkle in the eye,
a gentle caress—
all of which comes from your generous bounty!

Keep all married couples in your care, Lord.
May their love be pure and their lives kept safe,
and may they always seek to do your most perfect will
despite their imperfect lives.

In Jesus' name,
Amen.

A PRAYER FOR
DIVORCED CATHOLICS

Lord of love and life,
I come before you
seeking wholeness
and holiness of life.

With reconciliation to my spouse
no longer possible,
I humbly ask you, Lord Jesus,
to strengthen my sense of dignity
and self-worth.

With a sense of regret,
disappointment, and failure—
toward myself and my family—
for no longer living my matrimonial covenant,
I place myself before you.
I ask for your grace,
that I may remain your instrument of charity.

With a heavy heart, I cry out to you, Lord.
Help take away my feelings of hurt and pain,
of sadness and disappointment.
Help me make good decisions
that reflect your holy will.

Through Christ, our Lord,
Amen.

A FAMILY MEAL PRAYER

Bless this food, Lord Jesus,
which comes to us from your generosity
to nourish us and quench our thirst,
to renew us and keep us growing
in mind, body, and spirit.

As we receive this gracious meal,
keep us mindful of all those
who go hungry in our world.

May we never stop praying
for those without a meal.
Give them the strength and courage
to seek and find the resources they need
to better their own and their families' lives
—all for your greater honor and glory.

Through Christ, our Lord,
Amen.

A PRAYER FOR MY PET

O God, Creator of all life,
how grateful I am to you
for creating my loving pet.

How well you know the comfort and joy
I receive through the unconditional affection
(pet's name) _____ gives me.

As I go about my daily tasks,
keep my pet safe and secure
under your protective hand.

When I return home each day,
may my pet greet me lovingly,
just as I was greeted yesterday,
and I pray will be again tomorrow.

When my pet passes,
may I remain grateful
that you trusted me to care for
such a precious part of your creation.

Amen.

A PRAYER FOR PARENTS WITH CHILDREN WHO FACE CHALLENGES

Dearest Jesus,
I seek your help, in this, my hour of need,
because I feel desperate with the challenges I face
as the parent of this child.

Provide me with the courage and strength
that only you can give,
so that my anger may be replaced with hope,
my fear with confidence,
my indifference with zeal for life.

Grant me the wisdom
to see things as you do
and to accept the things I cannot change.

With your Holy Spirit as my guide,
may I move forward
convinced always of your love for me.

Amen.

A PRAYER FOR
A SINGLE PERSON

Jesus, my Lord and my God,
bestow your abundant grace upon me
as I commit myself to you and
your desire to bless me with a life as a single person.

May my entire life be one of praise and thanksgiving
for the many benefits and blessings
you so generously bestow on me.

Provide me with the necessary desire
to trust in you with all my heart.
Remind me often of your promise
to direct my path (Proverbs 3:5-6).

Teach me to walk always in your love,
never doubting your constant companionship.
Give me the disposition I most need
to conform all my desires to yours.

Through Christ, our Lord,
Amen.

A PRAYER FOR PARENTS WHO HAVE HAD A MISCARRIAGE

Jesus, our Lord and Savior,
we seek your comfort
during these difficult days of pain and loss.

We place the newest member of our family
under your gentle care
and into the arms of your providence.

May our little one,
already blessed by the natural gift of life,
now be embraced in your merciful arms.

Keep our child safe
until that day when we are reunited
in your eternal home, Heavenly Father.

In the days ahead,
comfort us in our grief.
May we remain faithful to one another and to you
all the days of our lives,
until we dwell in your house forever.

Amen.

A PRAYER FOR
A DECEASED SPOUSE

Heavenly Father,
look graciously upon me
during my hour of sorrow.

The days pass differently,
as never before.
Love for life is nearly impossible
in this time of heartache and grief.

Preoccupied by sadness and
feelings of emptiness,
my entire being aches
from the inside out.

And yet, I somehow know
that within your great providence,
all will be well in the long run,
as long as I place my complete trust in you.

I surrender myself to you
during this painful time,
and I renew my commitment
to pray for my spouse
as I, too, wait in joyful hope
for the coming of my Savior,
your Son, Jesus Christ.

Amen.

GOOD AND GENEROUS GOD

A PRAYER ON
THE DEATH OF A FRIEND

Dearest Jesus,
I always depend on your love and mercy,
but now my heart is overwhelmed with sadness
as I mourn the loss of my dear friend.

Only you, Lord, can offer the counsel I seek
during this unexpected moment in my life,
as I struggle with feelings of deep grief and sorrow.

Bless me with signs of your love.
More importantly, bless my friend as you welcome
    him/her into your eternal home.
In your kindness, provide all necessary
    comfort and sustenance
until we meet again in the joy of your heavenly kingdom.

Through Christ, our Lord,
Amen.

A PRAYER FOR MOURNING
THE DEATH OF A CHILD

Jesus, Lord of Life, watch over us in our grief
as we mourn the death of our beloved child.

May your Holy Spirit, who first gave our child life,
[and later provided new birth through baptism],
now breathe new life into his/her soul,
so that he/she may complete his/her heavenly journey.

May your holy angels minister to us who remain,
and may our Blessed Mother watch over us
until that day when we, too, are called
to surrender ourselves to your divine judgment and mercy.

Keep us safe, Lord, in your care,
and with our dear child, always faithful.
May we never abandon your holy will.

Through Christ, our Lord,
Amen.

PRAYERS
for VARIOUS
OCCUPATIONS

A PRAYER FOR SEEKING EMPLOYMENT

Lord of the universe,
people have sought work from the beginning,
not only to contribute to society
but to also get the food,
shelter, and clothing they need to live.

Be with me as I look for a job.
May I demonstrate competency and trustworthiness
to potential employers.

Keep me focused, Lord Jesus,
that I may not lose hope.
If I am successful today,
may I be grateful in prayer.
If I am not successful today,
may I not lose hope for a better tomorrow.

I trust, Lord, that you will direct me to the right job
that will ultimately bless each member of my family.
I place all in your most capable and loving hands.

In Jesus' name,
Amen.

A PRAYER FOR BUSINESS OWNERS

Good and gracious God, Father of all,
instill in my heart
the qualities I need as a business owner
to do all for your greater honor and glory.

Following the advice of the Psalmist, who said,
"It is well with those who deal generously and lend,
who conduct their affairs with justice" (Psalm 112:5),
I ask for your help: may I follow that advice
and be an example, so others will do the same.

May I be a good role model for my employees
and have a work ethic that others can imitate.

Shower your choicest blessings
upon all those who labor to support their families.
Provide coworkers with a proper spirit of collaboration.
Give me the wisdom to know when to
    speak and when to listen;
when to act and when to remain neutral.

In Jesus' name,
Amen.

A PRAYER FOR FIREFIGHTERS

God, our holy Father in heaven,
watch over our beloved firefighters
as they journey each day into the unknown.

Give these men and women
the courage they need
to combat, on our behalf, fire and flame,
water and smoke.

May these brave firefighters "be strong in the Lord
and in the strength of his power" (Ephesians 6:10)
as they use every good skill
to provide safety to others.

Be their shield, O Lord,
as they face these daily dangers.
Protect them from every tragedy
all the days of their lives.

In Jesus' name,
Amen.

A PRAYER FOR LAWYERS

Good and gracious God in heaven,
create in me a faithful, hopeful, and loving heart,
filled with love for you and your blessed virtues.

Give me the strength of character
to do my best, faithful to your law
and attentive to the people you place in my path.

Guard me from all who might seek to cheat or defraud me,
and allow me many opportunities
to defend those who have been treated unjustly.

Grant me the wisdom to seek only your truth;
and may I always serve with the greatest integrity,
performing my duties with love, sincerity, and justice.

Amen.

+ Mary, Queen of Justice, pray for us.
+ Saint Thomas More, pray for us.

A PRAYER FOR EDUCATORS

Lord, Jesus Christ,
we call out to you, Good Teacher,
asking that you make us all the best of teachers,
following your example as "educator par excellence."

Help us to believe, love, and live your truth
as we contribute to the welfare of the world
and the work of extending the kingdom of God
through our efforts in Catholic education.

Recognizing that the nursery of Christian
    life is the Catholic home,
while its stronghold is the Catholic school,
our hope for education is based on our Savior's desire:
    ...to learn the truth,
    ...to live the truth,
    ...to love the truth, and
    ...to share it with others.
Help us to treasure Catholic education.
Make our schools living communities
filled with your Spirit and teachings.

By our constant interest and abiding love,
may we as educators feel,
as in reality we are,
a vital and valued part of the whole people of God,
second only to parents, who are the first and
most important teachers of their child.

We hold up all who share our hope for education
and ask your special benediction
upon us and all our school families.

In your most blessed name,
Amen.

A PRAYER FOR THOSE WHO FISH

God of land and sea,
watch over all men and women
who fish for their livelihood.

Be generous to your servants,
as you were long ago to the chosen ones
who fished the waters of Galilee.

May those who cast their nets
and set their fishing poles
be likewise pleasantly surprised by their catch.

Bless your servants who fish
with the confidence of mind and heart
to prudently fish the waters
you have generously given.

May they recall often your tender presence
afforded the fishermen in the gospels
and be similarly bold in their resolve
to proclaim your word
and become fishers of people (Matthew 4:19).

Through Christ, our Lord,
Amen.

A POLICE OFFICER'S PRAYER

Good and gracious Father,
watch over me daily, and
watch over all my coworkers in blue—
including all who belong to our benevolent association.

Impress upon those in our society
our commitment to service and community outreach,
especially to those with special requests and needs
and those who are most vulnerable.

Give me and all my brothers and sisters who wear the uniform
hearts and minds after the example of Jesus.

May we realize our exalted position
in the cities and towns we patrol.
May we acknowledge, too, the rights of all—
those with whom and for whom we serve,
here in this place
and in every city and town throughout the world.

We ask this through Christ, our Lord,
Amen.

+ Saint Michael the Archangel, pray for us.
+ Mary, Queen of Peace, pray for us.

A PRAYER FOR POLITICIANS

Lord of heaven and earth,
watch over and guide our political leaders
and all who govern us.

May the truth of your gospel
penetrate the hearts and minds
of those chosen to lead us.

May these men and women
always seek to walk in your way
and lead us in the direction of life and love.

Help your chosen servants
be noble witnesses to your commandments
and become solid in their faith and moral lives.

Provide them with the necessary grace and wisdom
so they may never waver in their love for you
or for the people they are called to serve.

Through Christ, our Lord,
Amen.

A PRAYER FOR THOSE
WHO SERVE IN THE MILITARY

God of love and peace,
we approach you on bended knee,
asking your blessing
on all who call on your holy name.

Grant your sons and daughters
who serve our country in uniform
your divine protection.

Watch over our military families, too,
with your special favor.
When they are alone and afraid,
give them the grace they desire
to remain vigilant,
filled with the precious virtue of hope.

To all who enjoy living in a country
and worshipping a God who bestows on us
the special gifts of freedom, justice, and truth,
may we never take these rights for granted
but cherish them with humility and pride.

Through Christ, our Lord,
Amen.

A PRAYER FOR
MEDICAL PERSONNEL

Lord God, divine Physician,
be a source of kind and merciful assistance
to all medical personnel.

May the doctors who tend
to the needs of their patients,
the nurses who assist them,
and all EMS workers
be always mindful of their high call
to offer their best
to those who depend upon them.

May they always seek your support
as they attend to the health
of our brothers and sisters.

May they always balance care with cure
in their goal to provide
the best medical attention to all.

May they grow to love you more
as they share their love and attention
with and to the best of your creation.

As they offer their knowledge and skills
in their service to others,
may they treat each patient as another Christ,
even as they become Christ for their patient.

In Jesus' name,
Amen.

A DOCTOR'S PRAYER

My Lord and Savior, Jesus Christ,
I surrender myself to you each day
as I go about attending to my patients:
those who come to me in clinic
and those I visit at the hospital.

I pray that I may imitate you,
great and perfect Physician.
Give skill to my hands.
Sharpen my mind.
Provide me with clear vision
and a loving heart
in my dealings with those who seek healing.

May I always give care to my patients
as they seek a cure
for so many different ailments and diseases.

Lead me in all ways
so that my every waking hour will be focused on you.
Keep me faithful to the moral law,
that I may never take shortcuts as I attend to patients
and never compromise the Hippocratic Oath
that I committed myself to when I first became a physician.

Through Christ, our Lord,
Amen.

+ Saint Luke, physician and evangelist, pray for us.
+ Our Lady of Fatima, pray for us.

A NURSE'S PRAYER

Lord, holy Father,
you called me to your service
to use my gifts and training
as professionally as possible
for those in need of care and healing.

Keep me safe in your service
as I go about fulfilling my duties,
not only as a nurse to my patients,
but as an example to my peers
and as a reliable assistant to doctors.

Gracious God,
may I always do the best I can,
offering the finest health care,
medical competence, and comfort
to those who hurt and suffer
and all in need of healing.

Through Christ, our Lord,
Amen.

A PRAYER FOR A CAREGIVER

My Jesus,
your words from the gospel
ring out loudly each day
as I go about my daily duties
caring for this child of God:
"Just as you did it
to one of the least of these…
you did it to me" (Matthew 25:40).

Yet, much of what I do
seems mundane, unimportant—
sometimes boring, just routine.

Still, I know that the circumstances of life
have placed me where you want me to be,
giving my time and energy to another;
offering your care and comfort
through the work of my hands.

Gentle Lord,
teach me greater patience and understanding.
Help me show your love.
Console me in the knowledge that,
in spite of myself,
this opportunity affords me
everything necessary
to serve you most perfectly.

In Jesus' name,
Amen.

A COLLEGE STUDENT'S PRAYER

Jesus,
"the Way, the Truth, and the Life" (John 14:6),
bless me in all my pursuits,
especially in my studies.

Keep me focused and
especially aware of my need
to grow in greater knowledge
and understanding of
the subjects I am studying.

Help me if I become impatient
or tend to be lazy or procrastinate
and at those times when I become bored.

As I prepare for each new semester,
keep me focused, dear Lord,
    ...in my research,
    ...as I write papers,
    ...study for exams,
    ...give presentations, and
    ...participate in team projects.

May I embark upon my studies
in a spirit of collaboration,
helping others when I can.

May I always turn to you, Lord,
to seek success in my studies
but, more importantly,
to grow in my love for you.

Amen.

AN ACCOUNTANT'S PRAYER

God of all,
open wide your comforting arms,
and in your compassion hear me.

My days are filled with thoughts of money,
fixated on numbers and figures,
as I attend to the financial needs of others.

Whether I'm dealing with business or personal matters,
within or outside of tax season,
I ask that you help me attend to my obligations,
never envious, with the humility of spirit
that comes only from you.

May I always find comfort in your invitation
to seek first your kingdom,
and all else will be afforded me.

Through Christ, our Lord,
Amen.

A FARMER'S PRAYER

Lord of heaven and earth,
keep the soil of the earth
rich and abundant.

Whether we receive rain or sun,
may the balance of nature
always remain intact.

May the seed that is sown
become food for the multitudes,
a harvest that is plentiful,
never wasted, always shared.

Keep me always determined
to work the fields consistently,
never to waver in my love of nature,
maintaining and appreciating
the fruit of the earth
all the days of my life.

In Jesus' name,
Amen.

A VETERINARIAN'S PRAYER

Lord of all creation,
each day as I treat the needs
of my four-legged and other patients,
may I remain focused
in the knowledge that all I do
is not only for the comfort of my patients
but also for their two-legged owners.

While attending to the needs
of felines and canines, birds and reptiles,
keep me always aware of my special vocation,
attending to the pets that give so much comfort
to the best of your creation.

May I meet my obligations
with sincerity and professionalism,
offering care and attention,
and comfort when necessary,
to your greater honor and glory.

Amen.

AN ATHLETE'S PRAYER

God of all humanity,
be near to me in all that I do
to prepare my heart, mind, and spirit
for the challenges ahead.

May I be the best possible athlete,
building my body in a balanced, healthy way,
unafraid to reach my potential
using my God-given gifts well.

May I do nothing that brings disrespect
to myself, my teammates, or my opponents,
using all of who I am
to give you praise and thanksgiving.

When things become difficult,
as they sometimes do,
keep me safe and secure in the knowledge
that I do all things for your greater honor and glory.

In Jesus' name,
Amen.

A LIFEGUARD'S PRAYER

As the days of spring begin to fade
and signs of summer appear,
I am asking, Lord, that you keep me fixed on my call
to keep the preciousness of human life
    uppermost in my mind.

As a guardian of life, watching from the water's edge
for any sign of fright or flight or distress among my charges,
I pray that I never become passive in my duties.

May I rest well each night,
so that I remain vigilant each day.
Never allow me to become complacent,
because being a lifeguard is more than a job.
It is also a perspective,
highlighting the beauty and dignity of every human life,
made in your divine image and likeness.

Amen.

A PRAYER FOR TRAVELERS

Lord of all, send your Holy Spirit
to watch over us as we prepare
our travel plans and vacation destinations.

For those using the roads and highways
of this great land, we pray, on their behalf,
that they may enjoy your divine protection.

For those traveling in the air or on the water,
we pray for their secure passage.
May your merciful presence grant them respite
and refresh them on their journey.

May all who travel this day
arrive safely at their destination
knowing that you have protected them
from accidental and deliberate harm along the way.

Through Christ, our Lord,
Amen.

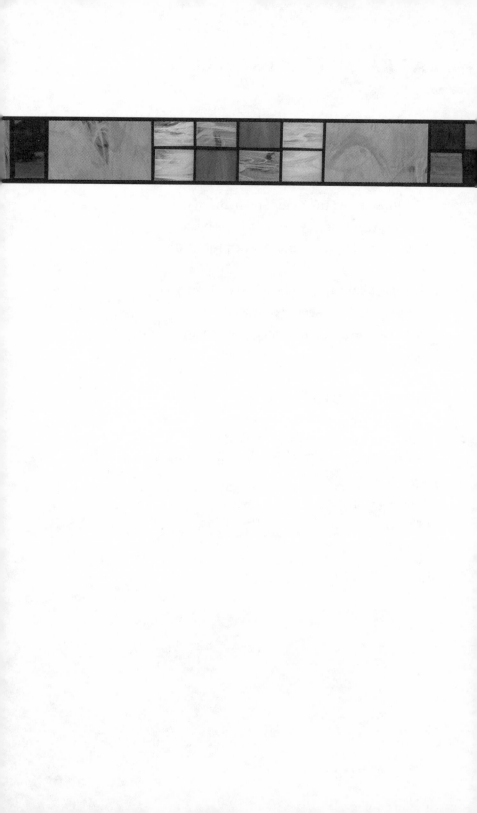

PRAYERS *for* *a* PEACEFUL WORLD

A PRAYER FOR PEACE

Jesus, Prince of Peace,
watch over your human family.
Keep us safe in your care.
When we are weighed down
by threat and adversity,
send your saints to intercede for us.

Into the world of politics, Lord,
send your Holy Spirit, our advocate,
to breathe new life into those
whose lives have turned away
from your hunger for
authentic peace and justice.

Within the interior lives of citizens, Lord,
provide spiritual awakening and genuine ascent
toward your incomparable desires of virtuous living,
free from distraction, disturbance, and dislike.

To those whose lives have turned from you,
rekindle in their souls and awaken in their minds
the joy of loving you and serving you.

Keep the path to peace foremost in their hearts.
Use every circumstance that is theirs
for your divine purposes
so that peace will become a reality.

Through Christ, our Lord,
Amen.

A PRAYER FOR
THE ENVIRONMENT

God of all creation,
abide with us in our present obligation
to preserve our earthly home
in keeping with your will.

Help change hearts and minds
to follow your intended design for our world.
Enable us, your servants, to identify
and offer direction to those who are a menace
to its legitimate care and advocacy.

May we each be reminded to be good stewards
who are genuinely attentive to the care of the environment
and to the authentic role we must play
in resisting any exploitation of our environment.

Help us, Lord, as your sons and daughters,
to be personally accountable,
caring for the place we call home
and providing an example for others.

In Jesus' name,
Amen.

A PRAYER FOR PEOPLE
LIVING IN POVERTY

Good and generous Father,
abide with those who live in sorrow and poverty,
that they may find in you the strength
to bear their misfortune while seeking
to overcome their difficulties and hardship.

Bless them with your divine favor,
that they may enjoy respect as children of God and
that they may rise above their present circumstances
with the help of many among their
      brothers and sisters in Christ.

Keep them close to you, Lord,
as they take action each day to find greater prosperity,
not only through the kindness and charity of
      others, and the fruit of their own labor,
but also through changes in business and
      government policy when necessary.

May all your faithful people
take the time and effort to seek and find
those most in need, both materially and spiritually,
and do our part to help lighten
the sorrow and poverty of people both here and abroad.

Through Christ, our Lord,
Amen.

A PRAYER FOR
A PEACEFUL CHURCH

Christ our Savior, watch over your Church always,
but especially during these turbulent times,
as we witness assaults on your holy Church
from within and without.

Recognizing the reality of human sin,
may all members of your body
be ever mindful
that every sin committed
is a sin against you and your body, the Church.

May we behold your precious Church as she truly is—
your mystical body and your beloved spouse—
and may we honor her as you honor her,
all the days of our lives.

Through Christ, our Lord,
Amen.

A PRAYER WHEN FACING NATURAL DISASTERS

Good and gracious God, Lord of the universe,
be our companion and guide
during these days of harsh and unpredictable weather.

We pray with diligent hearts,
depending on your providential care,
even as we battle the difficult times ahead for us.

For the sake of the vulnerable elderly and the wee ones,
may the winds subside quickly
and the rain wash the dust away.

May the brilliance of your blessed sun
shine its rays brightly on the horizon,
and may the light of the moon
penetrate the darkness of night
so that we may once again find solace
in knowing that you are the One
who cares for us always.

In Jesus' name,
Amen.

A PRAYER FOR THE ANNIVERSARY OF 9/11

Heavenly Father,
on this solemn anniversary of 9/11,
shine the light of your face
upon all who seek you
with sincere hearts.

We remember in prayer those who lost their lives
during those horrifying attacks
and those who later succumbed to the events of that day.
We ask your divine blessing upon their loved ones
and upon all who live in our sovereign nation.

Intercede for us, Lord God.
May we never forget.
Keep us safe and secure
against all dangers, foreign and domestic,
that threaten us and
the lives of all who call upon you
in faith, hope, and love.

Through Christ, our Lord,
Amen.

A PRAYER DURING
SOCIAL UNREST

God of all creation,
in your loving-kindness and goodness,
attend to our needs
during these most difficult and disorderly times.

Remove the hate that has taken up residence
in the hearts and minds of many.
Provide them with hearts and minds
that overflow with love for you and their neighbor.

In these days of social unrest,
give us the strength of character to offer
our many trials and sufferings for your
greater honor and glory.

Help us convince others along the way
that love can truly conquer hate once and for all…
if only we believe in your gospel of truth and light,
given to us through your Son's sacrifice on the cross
and his rising from the dead as he had promised.

In Jesus' name,
Amen.

A PRAYER FOR OUR PRESIDENT

God our Father, Lord of the Universe,
bestow wisdom and grace upon our president always
to fulfill this important role
with total submission to your perfect will.

During times of national upset and upheaval,
supply your choicest blessings,
that the deepest respect and affection
be shown to all people in our great land.

May our president be a world leader
who leads with a heart, mind, and soul
determined to show the greatest praise and honor
to your most glorious bounty.

Following the example of Jesus
—the Way, the Truth, and the Life (John 14:6)—
may we proudly hail our president
as one who seeks to fulfill these dispositions
according to your holy will.

Through Christ, our Lord,
Amen.

+ Saint Isaac Jogues, pray for us.
+ Mary, patron of the Americas, pray for us.

A PRAYER FOR WORLD LEADERS

Lord of heaven and earth,
watch over and guide our world leaders
and all who serve in government.

May the truth of your gospel
penetrate the hearts and minds
of all men and women in authority.

Help our leaders, servants of your people,
to be noble witnesses, attentive to their roles
as custodians of justice and liberty.

Provide them with the necessary grace and wisdom,
that they may never waver in their love for you
or the people they are called to serve.

May these men and women
always seek to walk in your way
and lead according to your direction
of life and love.

In Jesus' name,
Amen.

A PRAYER FOR
PERSECUTED CHRISTIANS

Loving God,
watch over your human family always,
especially those persecuted for being
consecrated to you through baptism.

May these, our brothers and sisters in Christ,
find consolation, not desolation,
as they bear the cross of our Savior.

May their heavy cost for believing—
torture, slavery, imprisonment,
and even death—
become the means for us to be ever more faithful.

May those caught up in the struggle to survive,
recipients of your consoling grace,
find comfort in your presence with them
to get beyond this time of trial.

May the intense suffering and terror
experienced by the new martyrs of this chaos
bear much fruit,
following the example of Jesus crucified.

Amen.

+ Saint Michael the Archangel, pray for us.
+ Saint Joseph, patron of the universal Church, pray for us.
+ Mary, Queen of heaven and earth, pray for us.